The Book of Cures

Dedicated to the healers of St. Martin, known and unknown,
from century to century and hospital to home.

Edited by Jenn Yerkes

Window to Another World

The book of cures is a small notebook from the 1800s. It was recovered from the remains of Pierre Beauperthuy's museum in The Old House in late 2017. The house had been unattended for some years following Pierre's death, and it was badly damaged during Hurricane Irma.

Much of Pierre's collection was still inside The Old House. It had been battered by the winds and rain, left exposed where the roof was torn open. Luckily, the notebook was one of the items that survived. In fact, it has survived many hurricanes since the first entries were written in it, perhaps 200 years ago.

This type of notebook is often known as a recipe book, receipt book or commonplace book. It collects valuable knowledge for a household. This often included remedies and other medical information. It could also include cooking recipes, household how-to guides, weights and measures, quotes and more.

Similar kinds of journals date back to ancient times, but this type of notebook was most common from the 17th to 19th centuries. Because of their value, many survived, at least compared to other types of document. They are studied by historians, and they offer unique views on the medicine, culture and history of this period.

Most studies of this type of document look at notebooks from Europe and North America. Major collections of these books contain hundreds of examples, but none from the Caribbean. This notebook offers a rare and exciting chance to study something new.

This book is also unique for St. Martin. Most available documents from this time period are official records and reports from people making a short visit. This notebook presents an entirely different kind of information about the island, written by someone who lived here.

Most of the notebook is used to record medical treatments. This was certainly valuable to have in the home. A doctor was a long ride away on horseback, for those who could afford a doctor. There was no guarantee that there would even be a doctor on the island at at all. At least, not the kind of European doctor that the author of this notebook consulted.

This unassuming notebook is a treasure trove of unique information about 19th century life on St. Martin.

By documenting cures, the notebook tells us what was ailing St. Martiners in the 19th century. It was a time and place where many diseases were deadly. Compared to today, death was all around. Infant mortality was high and life expectancies were low.

The state of medicine at the time was terrible by today's standards. The germ theory of disease—that microbes like bacteria and viruses cause infectious diseases—was not well-developed or accepted when this notebook was written. Scientists like John Snow, Louis Pasteur and Joseph Lister were beginning to understand germs and sanitation in the late 1800s, but it would take time for their ideas to become mainstream.

Available medicines were also limited. Antibiotics were not widely available until the 1940s, a century after this notebook was written. The medical practices in the notebook are primarily rooted in European traditions. They have more in common with the alchemy of the Middle Ages than today's medicine.

Books like this little brown notebook can offer a unique look at culture for several reasons. Unlike most documents from this period, these books were often written by women. We don't know the author of the St. Martin book, but it is possible that it is one of the only surviving documents written by a St. Martin woman at this time.

These notebooks also show social and knowledge networks. The St. Martin book, like many, often includes the source of information. In the case of remedies, it is often Dr. Allaway. Other entries seem to match information from printed reference books. Places and patients are named. Indirectly, we can piece together part of the local social scene.

The notebook was found at The Old House in French Quarter. Formerly known as Spring Plantation, it has been owned by the Beauperthuy family since the 1840s. Pierre Beauperthuy created a museum at The Old House. The book was found there, but its original authors and owners are still unknown. Photo from the Pierre Beauperthuy Collection.

This book was also passed from one person to another. The first section of the notebook, which is the focus of this study, probably dates to the early 1800s. Later pages feature different handwritings and even a switch from English to French. We don't know the relationship between the different authors. It is highly unusual for a notebook like this to switch languages, but St. Martin has always been a very multicultural island.

This book comes from a very important period in the history of St. Martin. The first entries were written during slavery, and perhaps around the time of emancipation in the French colonies. Later entries by another author come after emancipation on both sides of St. Martin, a time often referred to as the Traditional Period.

The notebook does not directly address slavery and has just one mention of a man "belonging" to a particular estate. The notebook is clearly a product of the slaveholding class. As such, it tells only a small part of the story of St. Martin at the time. It doesn't offer the perspective of enslaved or formerly enslaved people that is so sorely missing from St. Martin's historical records.

In the remedies recorded, this notebook does contain hints of knowledge from St. Martiners of African descent. Certain recipes contain local plants, which may reflect African plant medicine traditions as practiced in the Caribbean. Perhaps the first recorded medicine by a Black St. Martiner is included, without credit, in this notebook.

Every page of this small notebook reveals something about life on St. Martin during a very different time. It was a time when most of the people on the island were enslaved and then finally free. It was a time when doctors didn't know about germs and prescribed poisons to their patients. It was a time when the place of women in society was radically different. It was a time when St. Martin was at the edge of empires, remote and forgotten. It was a time when the island moved from one era into the next, from a dehumanizing past through many hardships towards a brighter future.

20 grains 1 scruple Э
60 grains or 3 scruples 1 Dram Ʒ
0 grains or 24 scruples or 8 Drams 1 ounce Ʒ
5760 grains or 288 scruples or 96 Drams
12 ounces 1 Pound.

20 Grains — 1 scruple
3 scruples 1 Dram
8 drams 1 ounce
12 ounces 1 Pound or Pint.
a Tea spoonful of any liquid is considered
to be 1 Drachm 2 tablespoonful 1 ounce
a wine Glass full 2 ounces.

apothecary's signs.
Э a scruple   Ʒ an ounce
Эi one scruple
Эij two scruples   Ʒij two ounces
ЭΒ half scruple   ƷΒ half a dram
Ʒ a Dram   ƷΒ half ounce
Ʒii two drams

Doctor Allaways prescription for an
obstinate Fever.

15 Grains of Calomel, 9 Grains of antimonial powder, and 9 Grains of Camphor
made up in seven Pills, two Pills given
every two Hours for an adult, and for an
under age one every two Hours.

Inflamation of the Bowels.
15 Grains Rhubarb   made in 8 Pills one
15 Grains Camphor   Pill given every two
12 Grains Ipecacuanha   Hours.

Doctor Allaways powder given to children in
an obstinate fever.

60 Grains nitre   divided in 8 Powders
15 Grains Calomel   one given every two
1 Grain Tartar emetic   Hours.

Opening A Book of Cures

The little brown notebook is warped with water damage. It's small enough to fit into a coat pocket and about 100 pages long. Inside is local medical knowledge from a long time ago. It is all carefully written in script that is mostly still legible today.

On the inside front cover is a quick primer on the apothecaries' system of measurement: 20 grains in a scruple, three scruples in a dram, eight drams in an ounce. This is handy because most of the recipes for cures are given in grains.

One of the first medicines in the book is "for a swelling from cold." It contains 30 grains of calomel, a chemical containing mercury, and 40 grains of jalap, a medicine made from the powdered root of a type of morning glory vine. Both were fairly popular drugs in the 19th century, and neither are in common use today. These drugs were to be "made in 24 pills for a person 14 to 16 years, three pills given every morning."

Many of the medicines noted in the book are oddly specific, like this dosage expressly for people 14-16 years old. In fact, the very next cure in the book is for "the dry belly ache such as the woman Judy had." Many of the early cures are attributed to a Dr. Allaway. Some combine chemicals with plant remedies.

What is this odd book? Who wrote it? When is it from? The book contains a list of medicines sent to Lucas Percival. Percival was born in either 1789 or 1809 and died in 1877. He was on the local council of justice in 1829 and became Lieutenant Governor of the island in 1859. This, and other clues from the text, show the book was probably started in the early 1800s.

Later in the book, though, the handwriting changes and the language switches from English to French. This shows the book was passed on to another author or authors. Dates mentioned at the end of the notebook are at the end of the 19th century.

The cures themselves are mostly not things one would recommend today. Many include things we now know are poisons, like mercury and lead. This little book is a unique window into the hardships of life on St. Martin in the past. It tells us what ills bedeviled residents at that time. And it tells us that doctors had little to offer that would help. Back then, medicines were mixed at home from ingredients ordered from New York, and it was wise to write down medical recipes in case a doctor wasn't around for the next obstinate fever or case of jaundice.

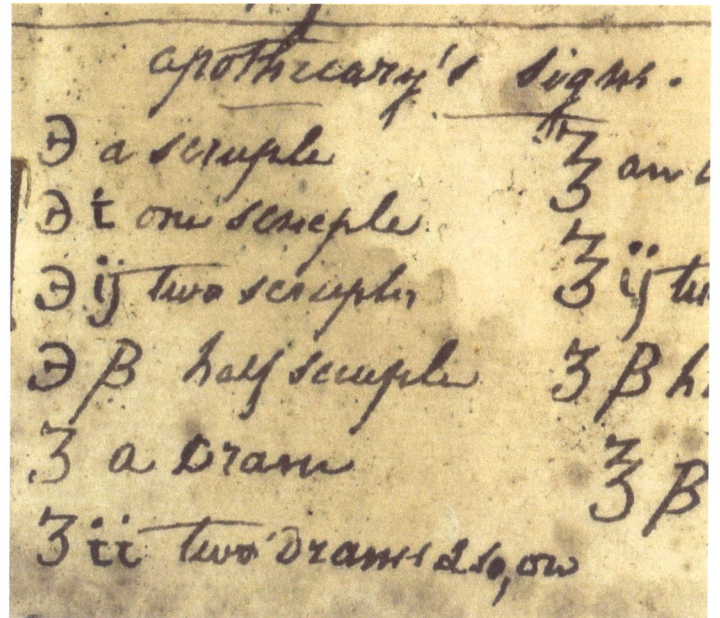

A key to the symbols used by apothecaries was written on the inside cover of the book. Although these symbols weren't used in the recipes in the rest of the book, this key may have been used when consulting other sources that did use them.

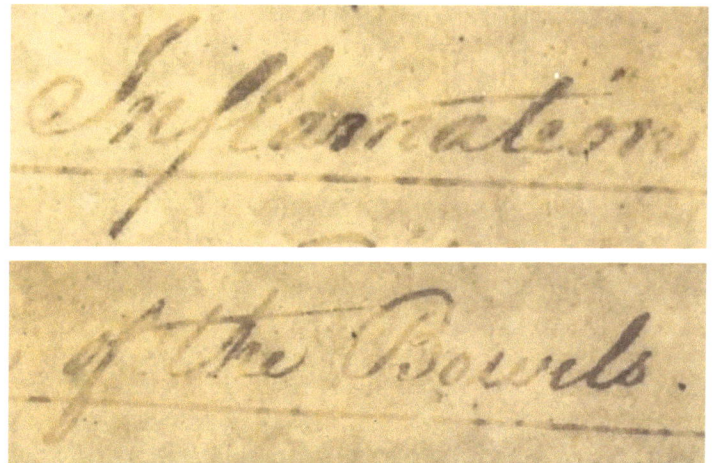

"Inflamation of the Bowels" was a malady that appears several times over the course of the notebook. It is referred to by several different names and several different remedies are presented for it. It is perhaps unsurprising that gastrointestinal problems were common in the era before refrigeration.

◄ *Ipomoea purga, a kind of morning glory vine known as jalap, used to create the medicine also called jalap. Illustration by an unknown artist, 1890.*

For a swelling from Cold.

30 Grains Calomel   made in 24 Pills for a
40 Grains Jalap.   Person 14 to 16 years, 3 Pills
      given every morning.

For the dry Belly ache such as
the Woman Judy had.

a table spoonful of Rhubarb
the same weight of aloes well
ground together & made in pills
of five grains each, & four or five
pills given every morning for four
or five days until the Bowels
are well evacuated

Copy of a List of Medicine which Mr. Lucas
Percival Sent for to New york, & which he
received in a Bill with the Prices.

			£	s	d
No 1	a Box				57
	5 lb Pulv. Creme Tartar	22			44
	4 oz Corros. Sublimate				44
	1 lb Gum Arabic No 1				38
	1 lb Salt nitre				11
	2 oz Opium Turkey	31			62
	½ lb Sugar Lead	28			14
	1 lb Comp. Epispastic				88
	2 lb Flo. Sulphur	7			14
	¼ lb White Vitriol				6
	¼ lb Blue Do				6
	1 lb Snake root long				56
	1¼ lb Sarsaparilla	40			50
	2 lb Cork Safafras	21			50
	1 lb Flow Chamomile				31
	1 lb Rad. Pentian				12
	1 lb Calamus				22
	2 Evans Lancets Case J	5/	1		38
2	a Box				31
	2 oz Calomel Vial 4	1/			29
	Carried over		£	7	83

Bad Medicines

If you lived in St. Martin in the 1800s, hopefully you didn't get sick very often. For that matter, if you lived in many places in the 1800s, the odds of getting good medical treatment were pretty slim. A visit to the doctor could easily leave you worse off than you were.

Near the beginning of the notebook, we find a number of medicinal substances used at the time. Many of them are recorded in a list of medicines ordered from New York by Lucas Percival. The list spans two pages and features several dozen items. Presumably the chance to stock up a 19th century pharmacy for a remote island in the Caribbean didn't come every day. It is the only list of its kind that appears in the notebook.

One of the first medicines on the list is corrosive sublimate. If you think it sounds bad, you are right. It is a white, crystalline substance made of mercury and chlorine. Mercury itself is very toxic, but this particular preparation is also corrosive. It burned the mouth, throat, stomach and intestines. In large doses it caused kidney failure and death. It was such a dangerous poison it was used to murder people.

Also on the list was calomel. Calomel is also made of mercury and chloride. Thankfully, it wouldn't burn you. But it would still give you mercury poisoning. It was used to make people vomit or evacuate their bowels. It worked because it was poison.

Sugar of lead was on the shopping list, too. Lead acetate is sweet, and was used as a sweetener and a medicine. But we don't use it today because lead is toxic. Also on the list was tartar emetic, which contains antimony. Its effects are similar to arsenic poisoning.

By comparison, other items on the list were not nearly so bad. Flowers of sulphur act as a fungicide and may have some uses. Opium can be abused, but we still use its active ingredient—morphine—as a pain reliever. Snake oil has become a generic term for fake medicine, but at least it didn't do anything, which is better than can be said for corrosive sublimate.

Rounding out the shopping list were a variety of plants and plant preparations: rhubarb, chamomile, camphor, sassafras, sarsaparilla, jalap, lavender and more. It is hard to say if they were used effectively, but most of these plants have some medicinal properties. Better still, they aren't deadly poisons.

Although medical science wasn't much of a science back then, western doctors had adopted some plant cures. Most of these came from other parts of the world with more developed plant medicine traditions. Some of the medicinal recipes in this book also combine purchased medicines with local plants. Perhaps European doctors on St. Martin were learning plant medicine from St. Martiners of African descent. And hopefully using that knowledge to provide better care.

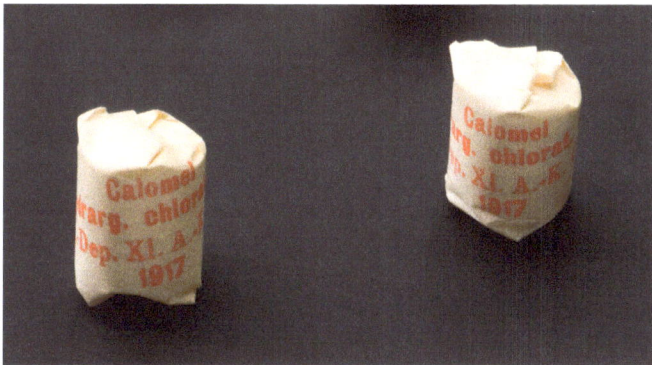

Some of the poisonous chemicals used as medicines in this notebook were later repurposed for other uses. For example, some were used as insecticides. This was probably a more appropriate use. These calomel tablets were produced in Germany in the 20th century. Photo: Science Museum, London.

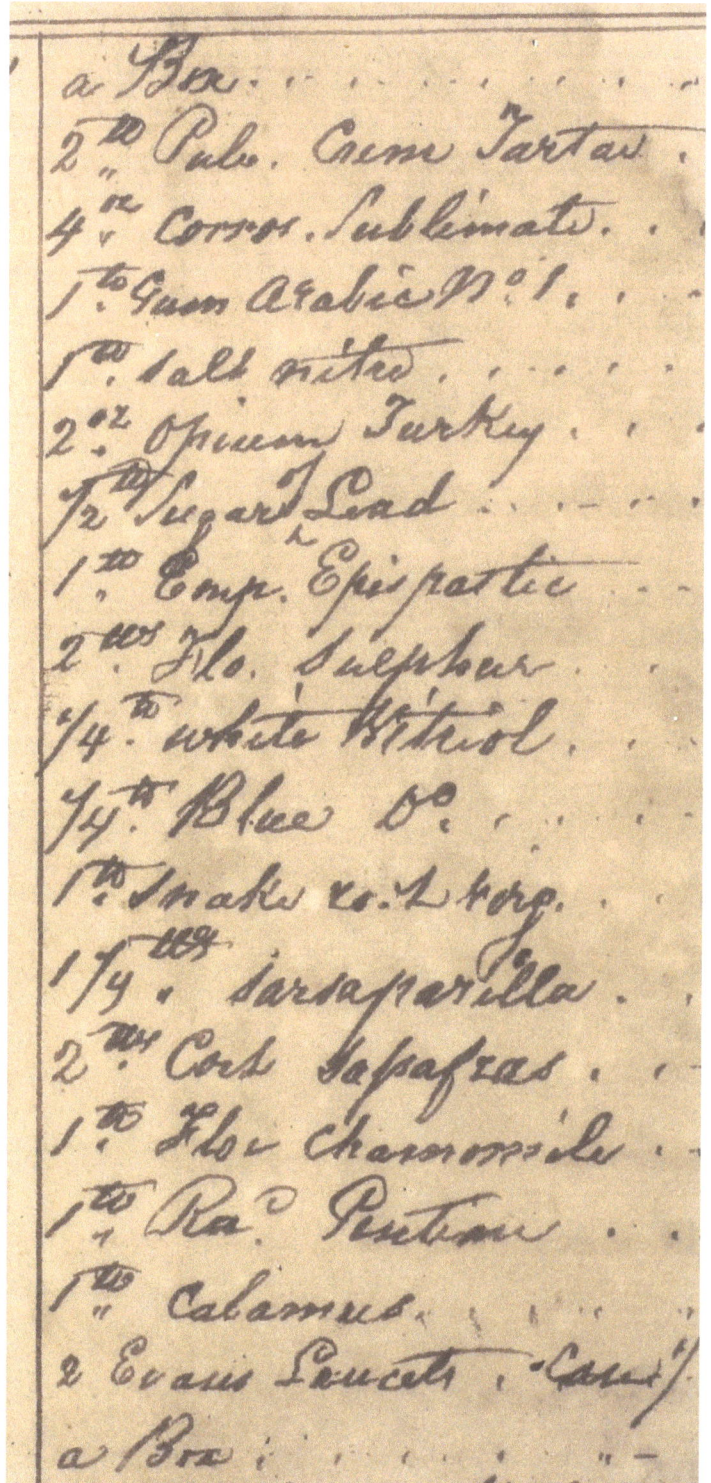

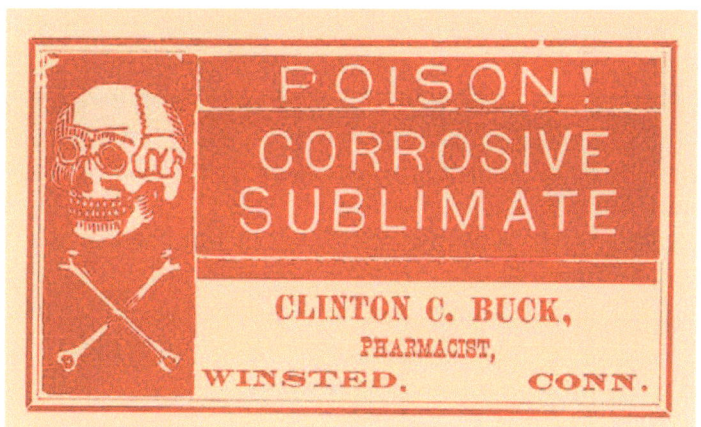

POISON!
CORROSIVE
SUBLIMATE

CLINTON C. BUCK,
PHARMACIST,
WINSTED.   CONN.

For a Young Woman...

On the fifth page of the notebook, there is an interesting entry. It describes a medical preparation "For a young woman who has not menstruated." The recipe is as follows:

> a large hand full of Doodledoo Roots, as much of Cankerberry roots, & the same quantity of Cashia roots, put with 6 pints of water, & boiled down to three, a tumbler taken three times a day, & plenty of exercise taken. a tablespoon full of Yucca in each tumbler of drink, & sweetened if necessary.

This medicine is different from most in the notebook. It is one of the only recipes that is entirely made of local plants. Doodledoo is a name still used for the columnar or candlestick cactus growing on St. Martin. Cankerberry can refer to a couple different plants on the island, the Bahamas nightshade and the rouge plant or jumbie basil. Cashia is another name for the acacia tree.

The exact purpose of this cure is unclear. Was it used when menstruation was delayed or irregular, which was seen by some doctors as a problem at the time? Was it for a young woman who had never menstruated? Or a young woman who had stopped menstruating because she was pregnant? It isn't clear from the text.

As far as we know, the cures in the book are actual remedies given to people on the island. In several cases, these people were named in the description of the remedy. In this case, we don't know who the young woman is. We also don't know her exact age, her background, or whether she was free or enslaved.

Was this medicine used to end pregnancies? There is a long history of abortion as a form of resistance for enslaved people. By not having children, enslaved people were able to hurt slaveholders economically and keep a future generation from suffering under slavery. The enslaved women who were midwives and healers also had some of the best knowledge about plant medicine.

However, this book was not written by an enslaved person. For economic reasons, a slaveholder would not want to end the pregnancy of a person enslaved by them. Abortion was also illegal and against the rules of the church, so it wasn't allowed for free people at the time, either. A recipe for this could be dangerous to have. This danger could explain why this condition was not described in detail, and why the identity of the patient wasn't recorded.

The plants used don't offer immediate clues, either. Cankerberry and Cashia both have plant medicine uses in the Caribbean and beyond. But there isn't clear evidence that they were used for anything related to menstruation, particularly on or near St. Martin. Perhaps further research can reveal more about this recipe and its purpose.

The Cankerberry (Solanum bahamense) is also known as Bahamas Nightshade. It grows wild on roadsides and in pasture and scrub areas. Illustration by N.J. Jacquin.

◄ *Doodledoo is a columnar cactus, Pilocereus royenii, that is native to St. Martin. Illustration by F.W. Horne.*

6) a Cure for the most obstinate
ulcer.

Yellow prickle wood water must
be used as a bath for the sore after
which you take the Bark of the yellow
prickle wood pounded and sifted
fine & the sore sprinkled with it then
apply over it a poultice of bread &
water.

Dimensions of the Cistern on the Estate
Golden Rock.
    14 feet long in the clear
    8 feet wide Do
    5 feet deep to the vent holes.
Calculation as follows.
    14 feet   8 feet   5 feet
     12   12   12
    168 Inches   96 Inches   60 Inches

          168
           96
        ──────
         1008
         1512
        ──────
        16128
                        60
    231) 967680 (4189 Galls equal to 38 Pun.

Doctor Allaway recommended for the
man Will belonging to Estate Mary's
Fancy who had a sore on the Leg. the
following 18 Grs of Calomel
            9 oz of opium
made up in 18 Pills wt a little soap
a Pill in the morning and one at night.

an excellent Poultice for breaking
a rising effectually. ─   ─
take the four o'Clock blossoms with
one or two of the young leaves. with a
roasted Potatoe (the middle of it) and

Important Information

We know a recipe book like this was precious. The book is full of cures, remedies and other medical preparations. These prescriptions by local doctors could be used by the notebook's owner if a doctor wasn't available. It is easy to understand why this medical knowledge would be valued. For other information, the value is less obvious.

A mathematical calculation is sandwiched between treatments for ulcers and a leg sore. It is for the "dimensions of the cistern at the Estate Golden Rock." Measurements in feet for the length, width and depth "to the vent holes" are converted to inches. These measures are converted into cubic inches to give the volume of the cistern: 967,680 cubic inches. The volume in cubic inches is then divided by 231 to give the number of gallons: 4,189.

This calculation could have been done on another piece of paper. Knowing the capacity of this particular cistern is not valuable to most people. But by recording the process of calculating the size of the Golden Rock cistern, the notebook can help anyone find the volume of any cistern. This formula could also be used to plan the size of a cistern to hold a certain amount of water.

On the other hand, this calculation doesn't record any wisdom about how big a cistern should be. Four thousand gallons is 22 gallons a day for a six-month dry spell. How many people could that support?

Cistern water was probably used only at the plantation house and by those who lived there. Virtually every estate also had a well. Most had small ponds for livestock, too. Water for the enslaved families and the rest of the plantation would have come from those sources.

Other non-medical information appears in the notebook. The eleventh page is labeled "Note from Mortimer's Commercial Dictionary." It contains instructions for planting, raising and harvesting tobacco, copied from the book *A New and Complete Dictionary of Trade and Commerce* by Thomas Mortimer. This book was written in 1766 and revised and reprinted a number of times.

Why was this particular passage copied? Did the notebook author have a chance to copy it directly from someone else's *Dictionary*? Was it a passage passed on from person to person? Tobacco had already been grown successfully on St. Martin for 200 years by the time this passage was written in the notebook, so why choose this information to save? Why not record information about how to grow sugar cane, the most important crop at the time?

We will probably never know why some information made it into the notebook. Perhaps some things that we might think useful to record were so widely-known at the time that it didn't seem necessary. Perhaps it was just chance that the writer had access to one bit of knowledge and not another. The fact that this collection of information is so personal and unique is part of its value and remains a source of mystery.

A NEW AND COMPLETE

DICTIONARY

OF

TRADE and COMMERCE:

CONTAINING

A Diſtinct EXPLANATION of the

GENERAL PRINCIPLES OF COMMERCE;

An ACCURATE DEFINITION of its TERMS;

AN

Ample ILLUSTRATION of the LAWS and CUSTOMS of all Commercial States, with reſpect to MERCANTILE AFFAIRS, in general; including the ſeveral TREATIES of COMMERCE actually ſubſiſting at this Time between the different Powers of EUROPE.

A Particular DESCRIPTION of the different

PRODUCTIONS OF ART AND NATURE,

Which are the BASIS and SUPPORT of COMMERCE;

Particularly diſtinguiſhing the

Growth, Product, and Manufactures of GREAT BRITAIN and its Colonies.

AN

Exact Specification and Valuation of all FOREIGN COINS, with Eaſy Conciſe TABLES for reducing them to the BRITISH STANDARD. An Hiſtorical and Critical Account of all Public and Private COMPANIES, and of all Public BANKS and FUNDS, with the Nature of their Securities. An Abſtract of the BYE-LAWS and CUSTOMS of all Ports and Harbours; with a Deſcription of the OFFICE and DUTY of CONSULS, AGENTS, and other Perſons reſiding in Foreign Parts, for the Protection of the Commerce of their reſpective Nations.

ALSO

Obſervations on the PRESENT STATE of our FOREIGN COMMERCE, and of the NEW MANUFACTURES eſtabliſhed and brought to Perfection of late Years in GREAT BRITAIN, of which no Account has hitherto been given in any other Commercial Dictionary.

By THOMAS MORTIMER, Eſq;

His Majeſty's VICE-CONSUL for the AUSTRIAN NETHERLANDS.

LONDON: Printed for the AUTHOR;

And ſold by S. CROWDER, at the Looking-Glaſs; and J. COOTE, at the King's Arms, in Pater-noſter-row; and J. FLETCHER, in St. Paul's Church-yard.

MDCCLXVI.

Printed books like Mortimer's Dictionary of Trade and Commerce often have a lot in common with the recipe books kept by families. In both cases, they contained a variety of valuable practical information.

A recipe for "the man Will belonging to Estate Mary's Fancy who had a sore on the leg" seems to tell us that this part of the notebook was written during slavery. It is also the only time we read about medical treatment given to an enslaved person, although we don't have details on most of the patients recorded in the notebook.

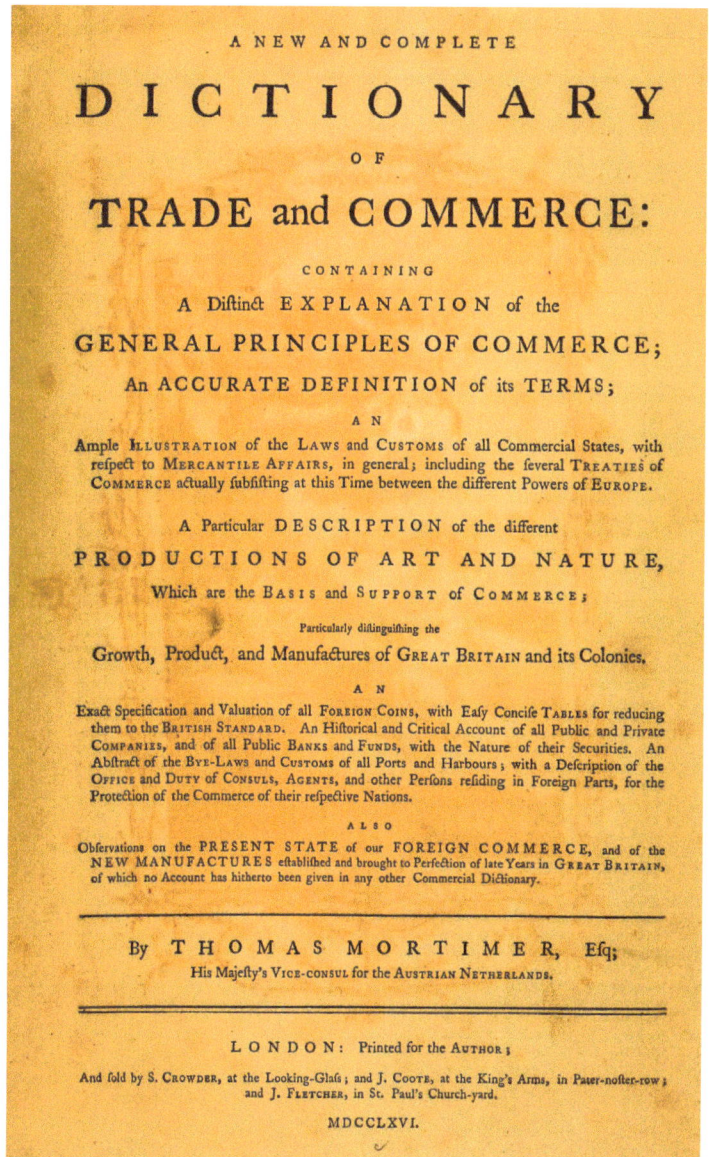

8/ some lard well stewed together
& placed on a Castor nut leaf and
applied — for a young child the flour
of lock beans, & blossoms but not ye
Castor with it

N.B. as ye Marsh Mallow leaves
may be put wt the roasted Potatoe
& your Clock

For the Flux, or Dyssentery.
First give an Emetic of Ipacacuana
then a dose of either Rhubarb, or Castor
oil, the next day commence with
the powders made as follows.

* 60 grs. Cream of Tartar
30 grs Rhubarb
20 grs Ipacacuana
the whole well rubbed together in a
mortar. To an adult 8 grains given three

times a day, and a Pill going to bed
every night whilst taking the powders
the Pill made thus

10 grains opium to 20 grs Ipacacuana
made in 10 Pills. The patients must
avoid eating any vegetable whatever, their
drink should be dry & nutritious the water
previously boiled and cooled should they drink
it, or if hot boiled a little toasted bread in the
water, Rice or barly Water is also
recommended but above all new milk to
be avoided the Patients kept from
damp or cold.

N.B. The powders should be taken,
not immediately after eating, or drinking
nor should any thing be taken after them
for an half hour at least, as they may
sicken which is not the intention.
* made in 12 powders for an adult & 16
powders for a child.

The Flux

Historical documents are often formal papers written by officials and preserved by the state. Much of what we know about St. Martin's history comes from records like these. Private documents, like letters and journals, are often lost over the generations. When they are available, they can open a whole new window into the past.

This notebook opens a window on a lot of stomach trouble. M.D. Teenstra visited St. Martin around this time and wrote a bit about the diet. He described a breakfast that was usually some combination of shrimp, lobster and fried fish. He said the afternoon meal was always fish, though prepared in various ways. We also know that people raised cattle, sheep and goats and grew a variety of crops like sweet potato, cabbage and guinea corn. Many of these foods could go bad when left out in the tropical heat.

The flux was a term for dysentery commonly used in the 1800s. The disease itself is an intestinal infection, often caused by Shigella bacteria. People were usually infected by drinking contaminated water or unrefrigerated milk. The disease usually causes severe diarrhea.

The treatment for flux is one of the most complex treatments recorded in the book. It starts by giving the patient "Emetic of Ipacacuana" which is essentially syrup of ipecac. This would induce vomiting, presumably to get the sickness out of the body. This was a common step in treating any disease of the digestive system.

Starting the next day, the patient would receive two medicines. During the daytime, they were given a powder three times a day. This powder was made from cream of tartar, rhubarb and ipecacuana. At night, the patient was to receive a pill made from opium and ipecacuana. Tartar and rhubarb were typically used as laxatives, and opium is a pain reliever.

Could such a cure be beneficial? Probably not. Since dysentery is an infection of the intestines, particularly the colon, vomiting induced by ipecac probably only increased the level of dehydration. The instructions even include a special note to avoid giving the patient the powder right after eating, "as they may sicken, which is not the intention."

Laxatives are also a strange choice to treat a patient that already has diarrhea. They could make dehydration even worse. Opium would help for pain, but also slows down the digestive system, which seems to counteract the other ingredients.

These medicines might not be great, but there were other instructions: "the patient should avoid eating any vegetable whatever, their diet should be dry and nutritive, the waters previously boiled and cooled." Boiling the water would make it safe to drink, and avoid reinfecting the patient. Rice or barley water was recommended, which seems helpful as well. The instructions also warn: "the use of milk to be avoided" and "the patient kept from damp or cold."

The flux was common at the time, so it makes sense to find a detailed treatment for it in this book. Patients that stayed hydrated and didn't get reinfected also had a good chance at recovery. This may be another reason why the treatment is so detailed. Perhaps it reflects a process of trial and error in developing and refining this method. By comparing this treatment to others from the same era, it might be possible to find out which parts were from medical training and which were developed on St. Martin.

At the time this notebook was written, European medicine was gradually progressing towards a science. This illustration shows the intestines of a person with dysentery. Illustration by C. Batelli, 1843.

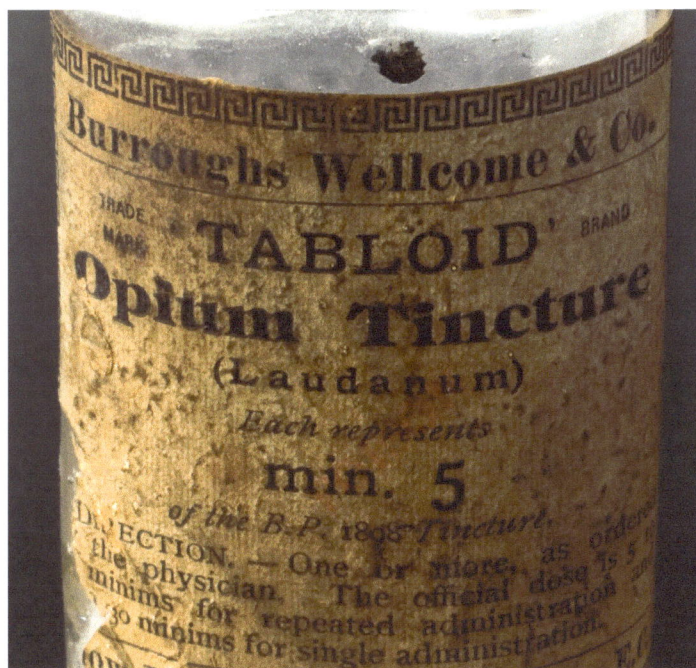

➤ A bottle of opium tincture. Opium was an important part of 19th century medical practice. It was one of the few medicines that worked, although it was often misused. Photo by Science Museum, London.

For dropsy

a large handful of bitter root stink
-ing weed,
d Ditto D° black dog root
a Ditto D° white candle wood root
3 quarts water boiled down to two
quarts a half pint given to an adult
three times per day with about an
ounce of good old rum in each dose
the patient to be well nourished and
well exercised all the while should
they complain that the drink operates
too severely the quantity must be lef-
=sened.

...

20 Gr Calomel
30 Grain Jalap
50 D° Rhubarb
120 Grain ... in 30 Pills.

a Note from Mortimers Commercial
Dictionary.

Tobacco must be planted after sow-
=ing the seed that they come up & have
at least six leaves to be carefully
transplanted 3 feet distance, and
allow the stocks to rise at 2½ feet
well suckered, free from weeds
to be 4 months growth, and cut down
to remain only one night in heaps
after being cut down, & then placed
over hurdles close covered, one industri-
=ous labourer can attend to 2500
stalks which ought to yield 1000 lb
Tobacco, & when fit to be reaped
the leaves become dark green

Local Plant Cures

Most of the recipes in the notebook are made from ingredients purchased abroad. Many of those compounds are things we now know are poisonous. Others were plant-based ingredients from around the world that had become part of European medicine of the time.

But the notebook also includes some remedies based on local plants. The source of these cures is not revealed, but plant medicine traditions in the Caribbean are rich. They come primarily from African and Amerindian cultures. Both groups have plant medicine traditions with roots going back thousands of years.

"A cure for the most obstinate ulcer" is one of these plant cures: "Yellow prickle wood water must be used as a bath for the sore after which you take the bark of the yellow prickle wood pounded & sifted fine & the sore sprinkled with it then apply over it a poultice of bread."

Cures made from locally-available ingredients would have big advantages over those that required imported chemicals. Imported goods were expensive and took a long time to arrive. It is not surprising to see local plants used in some cures.

"Four o'clock blossoms" and some young leaves are used in a poultice. For dropsy, a cure includes several plants: "bitter root stinking weed," "black dog root" and "white candle wood root". A tea to break a fever was made from "stinging windroots" and "black dog root."

It is not always possible to identify the plants in these recipes. Black dog root may come from *Senna bicapsularis*, which is still known as black dog bush in the Lesser Antilles. It is also still used in plant medicine. *Zanthoxylum martinicense* is a tree that is still known as yellow prickle. The name yellow prickle also appears in a poem by St. Martin author Laurelle "Yaya" Richards, where it is used for coloring. Four o'clock is a local name for *Mirabilis jalapa*, which is not native to St. Martin, but may have been growing wild here by the 19th century.

Although many cures in the notebook are attributed to Dr. Allaway, these plant cures were not. It seems Allaway preferred his mercury and lead concoctions. A cure for stoppage of urine from Dr. Griffin of St. Kitts was made from plants: "chicken weed root" and "white nicker root." The transfer of knowledge from Black Caribbean people to white doctors was surely different from island to island and doctor to doctor.

By the time this notebook was written, the population of St. Martin was mostly people of African descent, both free and enslaved. They had brought a rich tradition of plant medicine from Africa, and even many of the plants themselves. The most skilled healer on the island at the time was probably one of these people, although we don't know their name or have a record of their work. They may have used dozens or even hundreds of local plants. Although their cures may not be in this book, some of them have survived to this day via oral traditions.

Cassia fennoides
Jacq. Misc. vol. 3.

Senna bicapsularis is known as the black dog bush. Studies of this plant have found it contains a variety of compounds with potential medical uses. It is not surprising that this plant and many of its close relatives have been used in plant medicine in the Caribbean and Africa. Illustration by an unknown artist.

F. W. Horne

◄ *Called candlewood on some islands in the Lesser Antilles, Erithalis fruticosa is native to St. Martin and could be the "white candle wood" mentioned in one of the remedies. Illustration by F.W. Horne.*

A Warm Bath

Jaundice is a yellowing of the skin and eyes. It is caused by a buildup of a compound called bilirubin. The liver normally breaks down bilirubin, so often jaundice is a sign of liver problems. Common causes can include liver damage from alcohol abuse or viral hepatitis.

In the 19th century, doctors didn't known the causes of jaundice. There was an epidemic of jaundice—probably hepatitis E—in Martinique in 1858. On St. Martin, people probably developed jaundice for a variety of reasons. The notebook contains a treatment for it:

For Jaundice

Rhubarb 2 drams
Castile soap 1 dram
Oil of annis 12 drops rubbed together & made into 18 pills two taken night & morning & a warm bath every other night going to bed, it is necessary to take exercise.

Rhubarb, castile soap and anise oil are all common in prescriptions from European doctors at the time. Unlike some treatments, none of the ingredients are actual poisons. But the rest of the treatment is more interesting than the medicine.

Bathing became more common over the course of the 19th century, but for most people it was still rare. The resources required to take a warm bath would have been exceptional at the time on St. Martin. One would need a cistern with plenty of water, a tub, and people to draw and heat the water.

This is one of the clearest signs of status and wealth recorded in the notebook. The person receiving this treatment would have to be a wealthy planter, or a planter's family member. Depending on the time this was written, they were either a slaveholder or controlled a workforce of formerly enslaved people. They were part of a tiny group of people living in some comfort. The vast majority of the people on the island worked to provide that luxury, but lived in poverty.

No one cutting cane or picking salt would have needed a reminder that it is "necessary to take exercise." Even less-wealthy white St. Martiners were doing plenty of hard physical labor at the time.

The very next treatment in the notebook is for pills "to act on the Liver." Perhaps they were for the same condition that caused the jaundice. The recipe for these pills also includes rhubarb and anise oil. But it includes mercury as well, which is highly toxic.

In 19th century St. Martin, wealth could buy many things. It could buy a warm bath every other night. It could buy a life free from manual labor. It could buy the medical advice of Dr. Allaway. But it couldn't buy health.

Rheum palmatum is a species of rhubarb sometimes called Chinese or Turkish rhubarb. The powdered root of this species has been used in Chinese plant medicine for thousands of years. Rhubarb powder was one of the items purchased by Lucas Percival and shipped from New York to St. Martin. Illustration by F.G. Kohl.

▼ This illustration of the Retreat Estate made by colonial surveyor Samuel Fahlberg in 1819 shows the relative luxury that was available to the richest few on the island.

14 a cure for worms —

three powders to be given three successive nights, each powder to contain 4 grs. filings of steel, 2 grs. Calomel, and 2 drops oil of Rue, & the fourth morning a dose of Castor oil —

Golard Water

2 Drams of Sal ammoniac or sugar of lead to a bottle of water.

this is not for the eyes but for swelling &c

Eye water

1 scruple of white Vitriol or Tin to 4 oz of Rose water, or Rain water Raw water is bad.

15 A new discovered Cure for Dysentery

a tumbler of good white Flour & water, as thick as cream, three or four times a day, or often as the patient may be thirsty, & perhaps there will be no occasion to use it the second day —

Tysan to break a Fever

Six stinging weedroots & half the quantity of black dogroots boiled together, and as will orange peeled & sliced up the decoction thereon hot several times, let it cool & made a common drink of — the root of the above must not be scraped —

A Medical Discovery

The information in this notebook comes from a variety of sources. Often, local doctors were the source. Their knowledge came from their training and presumably medical books they brought with them. Other material was copied from printed books, like Mortimer's commercial dictionary. Some cures are presented without citing their origin. In one case, a cure seems to be brand new.

The title of the entry is "A New Discovered Cure for Dysentery." This remarkable cure is: "a tumbler of good white flour and water, as thick as cream, three or four times a day, or often as the patient may be thirsty, and perhaps there will be no occasion to use it the second day."

It is a surprisingly simple cure. Seven pages earlier in the very same notebook, another cure for dysentery took up a page and a half. It required many ingredients prepared into powders and pills and given at intervals throughout the day and night.

The new cure was probably more effective. Dysentery is an intestinal infection that causes diarrhea. The new cure kept the patient hydrated while their body fought the infection. Starchy, low-fiber flour water could also help stop the diarrhea. By contrast, the old cure included ingredients that would make the patient vomit and have more diarrhea.

This flour water cure seems better than the many cures full of poisonous chemicals. It also seems a lot like drinking arrowroot pap, a thick, starchy drink made from arrowroot. Arrowroot was used as food and medicine by Amerindian people in prehistoric times. Drinking arrowroot pap for intestinal problems was already widespread long before this "new" recipe was written down.

This suggests the transfer of knowledge. On the same page, there is a "Tysan to break a fever." The French word tisane means herbal tea, so it seems knowledge was shared between French and English speakers. More importantly, the tea included local herbs: "stinging weed roots" and "black dog roots." Caribbean plant medicine came from African and Amerindian traditions. This notebook seems to show these traditions being adopted by Europeans.

Many of the cures in this notebook are credited to someone. Often it is Dr. Allaway, who owned a plantation in Colombier. The new dysentery cure and fever tea do not credit anyone. Perhaps this is because they were learned from an enslaved healer.

Though we may never know the exact history of these cures, it is interesting to see the adoption of cures that may reflect non-European healing traditions. The mixing of cultures and traditions makes the Caribbean a rich and vibrant place. The colonial system was largely dismissive of the knowledge and heritage of the people it exploited, but in this case perhaps they were able to learn a few things.

Maranta indica

Arrowroot (Maranta arundinacea) was an important crop for Arawak people in the Caribbean. They called it aru-aru, which may be the origin of the name arrowroot. The plant was used as both a food and a medicine. Some early colonists recorded Amerindian people using it to treat wounds, including ones from poison arrows. This is another possible source of the plant's name in English.

Medicinal use of arrowroot by both Europeans and Africans was common in the Caribbean in the 17th century. By the 18th century, it was also used as a starch in many foods, from an ingredient in bread to a thickener for soup.

By the early 19th century, arrowroot starch was boiled in water to make a thick drink known as pap. This was often given to babies and people suffering from digestive disorders.

Arrowroot illustration by an unknown artist, 1808.

▼ *After being dug out of the ground, arrowroot is washed, pounded in a large mortar made from lignum vitae wood and the starch is strained from it. In this image, a family is processing arrowroot. Photo courtesy of Alfonso Blijden.*

a Woman threatened with abortion.

Beat the white of an egg till very light, put it on cotton picked dry fine about the size of a small saucer, & dust some fine black Pepper over it, & tie it to the Navel. & the patient be Kept quiet

To extract the essential oil from Flowers. Take any flowers you like which stratify with common sea salt in a clear earthen Glazed Pot when filled to the top, cover it well and put it in a cellar, Forty days after put a crape over it to strain the essence from the flowers by pressure. bottle the essence, and expose it for four or five weeks to the sun & dew of the evenings to purify

it. one drop is enough to scent a quart of water.

For mending Coppers, or any broken kettle Boil a half pint of milk whilst boiling curd it with a little vinegar, beat up the white of an egg and then beat it well with the curd, after beating it a long time sprinkle in it a little very fine boiling lime, & take care not to let it be too dry when employed to mend any thing and it will last very long.

Another cement
Take a quarter oz. of Ising Glass & a Gill of high wines put the bottle up to the neck in a kettle of cold water boil it gently for half an hour strain it while hot, & when to be used put it in hot water to melt it, & lay it on with a camel hair pencil, it will even glue marble.

A cure for sores.   (Beware)
Take 2 oz. of sarsaparilla 1 oz. sassafras 1/2 oz. senna leaves 1/2 oz. liquorice root and

For Mending Coppers

Compared to today, St. Martin in the 19th century was almost unimaginably isolated. Goods shipped from Europe would likely take months to arrive. People needed to be far more self-sufficient in order to survive. They also needed to be able to make or mend the items they depended on.

Things like nails, horseshoes, tools and other necessities were usually made locally. Each plantation probably had a small forge on site. Blacksmiths, carpenters, coopers and masons were typically enslaved men. They were highly skilled and the operation of the plantation depended on their work.

The ability to repair equipment probably became more valuable over the 19th century on St. Martin. The sugar industry was in decline. Most plantations were losing money and could not afford expensive new equipment.

One practical recipe in the notebook is titled: "For mending coppers or any other broken vessel." In the Caribbean, a copper or boiling copper is the giant round vat where sugarcane juice is boiled down. They were heavy and very pricey. They were a key part of sugar processing. After the decline of the sugarcane industry, they were used to hold water. Often, they were placed around a well as troughs for livestock to drink from.

The recipe for mending giant metal cauldrons seems a bit odd at first. It requires boiling half a pint of milk, adding a bit of vinegar to make the milk curdle and then adding a well beaten egg-white. Next, one must sprinkle in a little "very fine boiling lime" and "take care not to let it be too dry when employed to mend anything and it will last very long."

Though it may seem strange, this basic recipe appears in books as curd cement. It is claimed to be waterproof and long-lasting, but does not seem to be something that would stand up to very high heat. Perhaps by the time this recipe was recorded, the coppers were already being reused for things other than boiling cane juice.

In today's disposable age, it's hard to say what seems more strange: a recipe for superglue made mostly from food items, or the idea of mending a vessel at all. But back when this was written, the recipe for a glue was as valuable as the recipe for a medicine. In fact, the very next item in the book is a recipe for "another cement" based on isinglass, a kind of gelatin made from fish swim bladders.

Boiling coppers of various shapes and sizes can still be found all over St. Martin and the Caribbean. Some have been repurposed to serve as troughs for livestock. Others are displayed as decorative pieces at carefully landscaped villas. A few are abandoned in the bush, perhaps in the same location they were last used long ago.

▼ Curd cement was one of over a dozen different cement recipes featured in The Druggist's General Receipt Book by Henry Beasley. It appeared in the "trade chemicals" section of the 1850 book.

Curd Cement. Add ½ pint of vinegar to ½ pint of skimmed milk; mix the curd with the whites of 5 eggs well beaten, and sufficiently powdered quicklime to form a paste. It resists water, and a moderate degree of heat.

For Improving Rum

This little notebook is full of old knowledge. In some cases, it hasn't aged well. New medicines have replaced poisons like mercury and lead. Some things are simply not that necessary anymore, like homemade glue. On the other hand, some information is timeless. Like how to make rum better.

There are some clues to suggest that this book dates from the early 1800s. This is a time when sugarcane was grown on St. Martin and rum was made from it. The sugarcane industry was not very successful here and it didn't last very long. But during this time, knowing how to improve rum was surely useful.

The first method starts with balsam of Peru. The instructions call for adding 35 grains—about a third of a teaspoon—for every five gallons of rum. Balsam of Peru is a resin made from the sap of a tree that grows in Central and South America. It was used as a flavoring, a fragrance and a medicine. Many people have an allergic reaction to it, so it is not widely used today.

The balsam of Peru was added after being dissolved or pulverized, and left in the rum for eight days. The next step was to construct a filter with a hoop, a flannel bag and charcoal. Impurities were removed by passing the rum through the charcoal. This is a process that is still done today to many spirits. The instructions specify that the charcoal should be made from white oak.

Charcoal seems to be a low-value item to import across an ocean, but if white oak refers to a local tree, it is unclear which one it is. Since white oak is used to make barrels, perhaps charcoal was made from old barrels.

Directly below these instructions, a second process is recorded under the simple heading "Another." This method starts with 30 tonka beans, well-pulverized. Tonka beans come from another South American tree, and they were also used as both a flavoring and a fragrance. The bean powder is to be added to a demijohn of rum taken from a puncheon cask and left in the sun for a day before being shaken and dumped back in the cask. A puncheon is a size of cask, about 85 gallons.

The next step is to take some gunpowder tea and a half stick of finely chipped licorice and steep them in boiling water, closed for "24 hours or even a day." This is then strained into the cask as well. The final touch is some burnt sugar to add color to the rum. Although the burnt sugar—or caramel—tastes bitter, only a tiny bit is used to color rum.

Is it possible to use these instructions to re-create the flavor of rum that was made in St. Martin 200 years ago? Perhaps, but it is probably not needed. Many of these steps, like using caramel for coloring, are still used in rum making today.

COUMAROU ODORANT.

The cumaru or Brazilian teak (Dipteryx odorata) produces the seeds known as tonka beans. This illustration is one of hundreds of botanical drawings made by Jean Théodore Descourtilz for the 1829 book Flore médicale des Antilles (Medical Plants of the Antilles).

◄ *Balsam of Peru is made from the resin of the tree Myroxylon balsamum. It was once widely used as a flavoring, an ingredient in perfumes, and in medicines. The balsam contains dozens of different chemical compounds. The tree that produces balsam of Peru is actually native to El Salvador. Illustration by an unknown artist, 1890.*

21

... as ¼ lb of best green powder tea, put in a
vessel ... a half lb of stick liquorice chipped
fine ... put on it a gallon of boiling water
cover it close for 24 hours on ... a day
when perfectly cold throw it in the cask
but not the tea leaves, then to colour it
take 2 lbs of best refined sugar burn it
& colour it with that.

Analysis of Soils.
The following is a method of analysing
soils for ordinary agricultural purposes:
Weigh a convenient quantity of the earth
to be analysed say one thousand grains
dried in the open air; dry the same before
a fire on paper, so as not to scorch the
paper, re weigh, and the difference will
be the moisture. Roast the residue re weigh,
and the difference will be the organic
matter. Pour a convenient quantity of
muriatic acid on the remainder; when
stirred and settled pour it off, and add
oxalate of ammonia; the precipitate will
be the lime. Mix the remainder with
water and stir it well when a little
settled pour off the turbid mixture
and the suspended contents are argil-

laceous, and the deposit siliceous.

For stoppage of urine by Doctor Griffin
of S.t Kitts.
⅓ of chicken weed root
⅔ of white nicker root boiled to a
strong decoction a wine glass every three
hours.

For Head ache by the French Doctor
Laquirrie.
1 ounce Cream of Tartar
½ ounce Flour of Sulphur
well mixed in powder a tea spoonful taken in the evening & morning
until it commences to evacuate the
patient. Then stop.

Doctor Griffin's Pills excellent
5 grs. Calomel
10 grs. scocine Aloes
1 gr. Ipecacuanna
divided in three pills for a dose such
to be taken when required even one at
night.

Analysis of Soils

During St. Martin's agricultural past, people had to understand the land. Much farming knowledge in the Caribbean was passed down from African and Amerindian traditions. These cultures had thousands of years of experience with tropical crops. Their methods are still used today, in kitchen gardens and provision grounds where food is grown for local use.

In this notebook, we find another approach to understanding the land. It is a description of a process of analyzing soil. The method is simple, and could be performed by anyone with just a few items on hand:

> The following is a method of analysing soils for ordinary agricultural purposes: Weigh a convenient quantity of earth to be analysed say one thousand grains dried in the open air; dry the same before a fire on paper, so as not to scorch the paper; re-weigh and the difference will be the moisture. Roast the residue, re-weigh, and the difference will be the organic matter. Pour a convenient quantity of muriatic acid on the remainder; when stirred and settled pour it off, and add oxalate of ammonia, the precipitate will be the lime. Mix the remainder with water and stir it well, when a little settled, pour off the turbid mixture and the suspended contents are argillaceous and the deposit siliceous.

By this process, the user can find out the relative amounts of moisture, organic matter, lime, clay and silica in a soil sample. These traits can help people understand the richness, acidity and drainage of soils. In turn, these factors can help determine which crops may grow best, or how valuable the land is for farming.

While the process for analyzing soil is given in detail, there are no notes about what the results mean. Were St. Martiners making farming decisions based on soil analysis in the 19th century? At the very least, we know they had some of the skills to do so.

M.D. Teenstra included some comments about St. Martin's soil in his 1837 book. According to him, the best soils for growing sugar were in the valleys and the flatter parts of the hills. These areas had brown soil mixed with gravel, about six to eighteen inches deep. He also described the land as too stony to plow, and severely damaged by salt left behind by the hurricane of 1819.

In the early 1950s, soil analysis was done here using more modern methods. As one could have done with the method in the notebook, organic matter and calcium carbonate were measured. Many other attributes were measured as well, like pH (the level of acidity or alkalinity) and the amounts of nitrogen and phosphate. A report was published in 1955 about the soils of St. Martin and the geology beneath them.

Soil studies in the 1800s may have decided which crop enslaved people were forced to cultivate: cotton, sugarcane or tobacco. The 1955 report told how well crops for the dinner plate and grass for livestock were growing in local soils. We could do better soil analysis today, but far less land is cultivated now. Frequent droughts and crop-eating invasive animals like monkeys and green iguanas may be bigger challenges than soil quality.

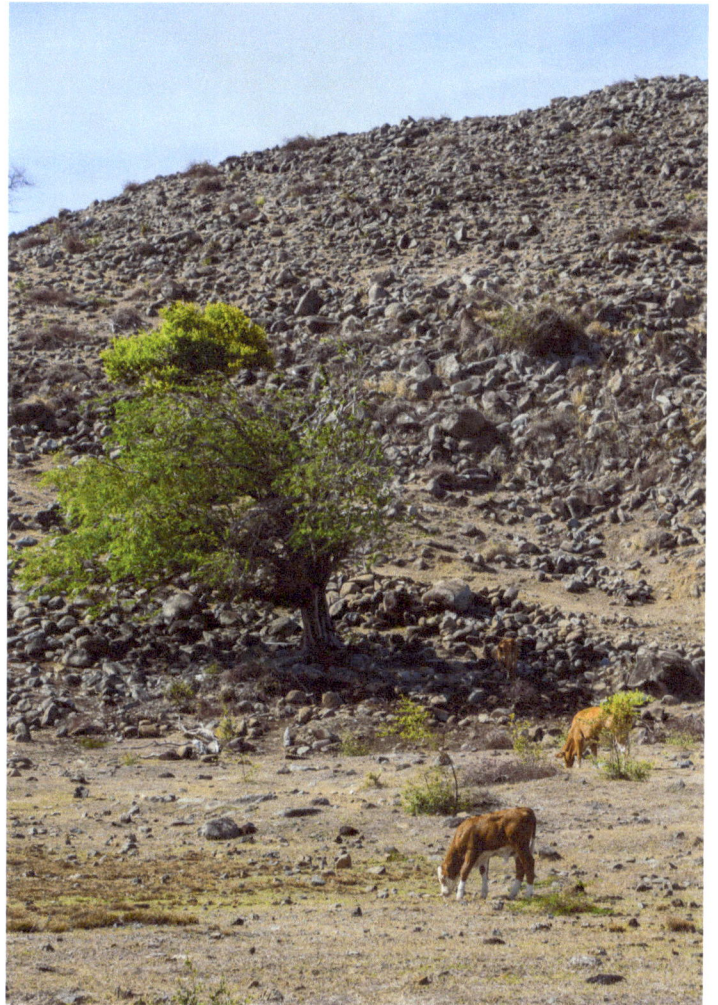

Fire and drought can reveal the state of St. Martin's hills: not much soil to analyze. Native forest was cut down to plant sugarcane and other crops. Over time, topsoil eroded away, leaving a natural cobblestone on many hillsides. The stony surface is hidden by grass during the rainy months.

Cure for the Locked Jaw

Lockjaw is a terrifying disease with a terrifying name. Also known as tetanus, it is caused by a toxin that is made by a bacteria. It causes a variety of symptoms, including muscle spasms that can be strong enough to break bones. It can kill, and in the past, it killed a lot.

Before modern medicine, tetanus was common in tropical areas like the Caribbean. Perhaps the warmth helped tetanus bacteria stay viable when lying dormant in tropical soils. Or maybe people just had more contact with the dirt and more opportunities to be infected.

In the little brown notebook, a cure for tetanus is described: "Make the wild tobacco in a strong bath, take out a little of it to make injections, which must be given frequently." This herbal treatment was combined with some of the popular medicines of the day: "Give the child two grains of calomel immediately, with a grain of antimonial powder."

This cure reflects another terror of tetanus: it was often a killer of infants. In the 19th century, when this cure was likely written, we did not yet understand germs. There was no vaccine for tetanus, and the umbilical cord was often a site of infection. Today, tetanus in infants is much less common. Most mothers are already vaccinated, which gives immunity to newborns.

Tetanus in infants usually kills in the first week or two. It killed infants of all backgrounds, but especially the babies of enslaved women. They didn't have access to clean water or clean tools and bandages for cutting the umbilical cord and protecting the newborn's navel area. Agricultural work put them in contact with soil, and the livestock manure used to fertilize fields. Both of these could contain tetanus spores.

At the time this cure was written down, perhaps a quarter of the babies born to enslaved mothers died in their first few weeks. Many more died as babies or children. Thankfully, infant mortality in the Caribbean has dropped over the last 150 years. Today, on some islands it is about the same as Europe or North America, though on others it is still two to ten times higher.

The handwritten cure for tetanus continues with a variety of other measures. Oil is taken to evacuate the bowels. Camphor, opium and candle grease are mixed together and spread along the spine, from the throat to the temples, and around the wrists. The bath and injections are repeated five or six times a day. "Remember to keep the child sitting in the bath until it appears sick at its stomach, but great care taken that it does not take cold."

Would any of this have worked? Probably not. Even today there is no cure for tetanus. The toxin created by the tetanus bacteria is one of the deadliest and most powerful toxins in the world. Both then and now, working to ease the symptoms during months of recovery is a big part of treatment. Luckily, today we are far less likely to get tetanus in the first place.

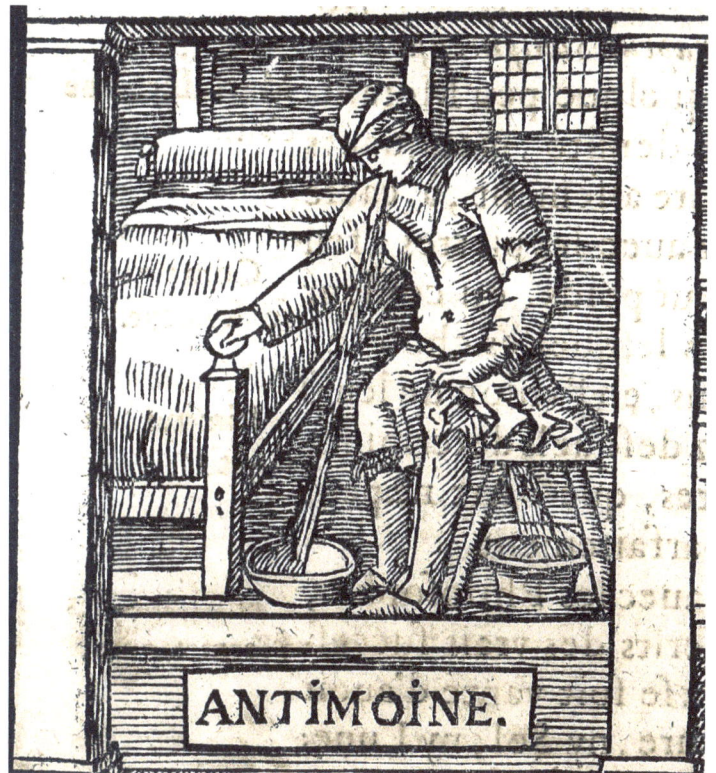

An early medical illustration shows the emetic (vomit causing) effect of antimony. Illustration by an unknown artist.

➤ *Pluchea carolinensis is one of several native plants on St. Martin that are known as wild tobacco. Cultivated tobacco, Nicotiana tabacum, was also an important crop on St. Martin and can still be found growing wild in some places on the island. Illustration by N.L. Jacquin, 1786.*

Cast of Characters

The knowledge stored in this notebook was valued by its author. For researchers today, the interactions between people that were recorded is often just as interesting. Many people appear in this notebook. Some are patients, some are doctors. Some are notable figures in St. Martin history, others we may never know.

Some remind us that there was a patient behind each treatment, like the woman Judy. She appears in the title of a remedy: "For the dry Belly ache such as the woman Judy had." Others invoke family names still common on St. Martin, like the pills prescribed for I.D. Gumbes "to act on the Liver."

Some tell a story of inter-island connection. A number of cures are recorded from a Dr. Griffin from St. Kitts, and one from "the French Doctor Laguionie." Some of these connections help us see why the island was never very French or Dutch, culturally. It was an English-speaking island, with close connections to neighboring English colonies.

Others help us place the notebook in history. One medical recipe was "recommended for the man Will belonging to the Estate Mary's Fancy." This seems to show that it was written during the time of slavery.

Early in the notebook is a list of medicines delivered from New York to Lucas Percival. He was born around 1809 and died in 1877. He is best known as the owner of the Diamond Estate in Cole Bay. Just after emancipation was announced by the French, 26 enslaved persons bravely left the estate to gain their freedom across the border.

This escape showed that slaveholders on the Dutch side could not sustain slavery as it was. Because of the resistance of enslaved and free people on St. Martin, these slaveholders were forced to make changes long before slavery was finally abolished by the Dutch in 1863.

Most of the cures in the first part of the book come from Dr. Allaway. Peter Welles Allaway was a surgeon who bought the Union plantation in Colombier in 1832. After French emancipation in 1848, Dr. Allaway was the first planter to sign a contract with free workers. Despite being a doctor, Allaway's contract has a clause noting that he makes no commitment to providing medical care to the workers.

The "Remedy by Parson Hodge of Anguilla for cough and digestion" is noted as "good." He is the Reverend John Hodge, who introduced Methodism to Anguilla and St. Martin. He was a free man of mixed race, with a Black mother and white father. He was also the first Caribbean person ordained by the Methodist Church. At the time, there was no doctor on Anguilla, so medicines were provided by the Methodist Missionary Society and care was given by missionaries.

One more name found in the book is not tied to the major historical changes in 19th century St. Martin, but is still important. Tucked at the bottom of the page is a short recipe: "Pills (by Doctor Allaway) prescribed by him for my daughter Anna Gumbes who had a catarrh, bilious fever and obstinate."

This is the only direct reference to the identity of the notebook's first author. It doesn't tell us if this author was the mother or father of Anna. So far, no record of Anna Gumbes has been found. But it may be in an archive somewhere, waiting to be digitized and put online.

"Monsieur le Commandant !" This urgent letter from the Dutch commander to his French counterpart is dated May 31, 1848, three days after emancipation was announced in French St. Martin. It requests the return of 26 people who escaped slavery on Lucas Percival's Diamond Estate to find freedom across the border. By choosing to take their freedom, these 26 people changed the nature of slavery on Dutch St. Martin for the fifteen years before it was abolished there in 1863.

These letters were added to UNESCO's Memory of the World Programme international register on October 30, 2017. Submitted by Sint Maarten archivist Alfonso Blijden, they appear in the global register as: Route/Root to Freedom: A case study of how enslaved Africans gained their freedom on the dual national island of Sint Maarten/Saint Martin.

Document from the Government Archives of Sint Maarten.

Rheumatism and Change

The handwritten recipe book looks fairly consistent for the first 25 pages. There are some variations in the ink and script, but the writing is mostly clear and legible. On page 26, things change.

A jagged line across the page marks the starting point of a "cure for Rheumatism." The letters are suddenly irregular, as if written by a shaking hand. Dark spots spatter the page where droplets of ink had accidentally fallen.

The recipe itself is similar to many that came before. Raw turpentine, castile soap and sulfur are combined and applied to the bottom of the feet. But this seems to be the last entry from this author. It is tempting to wonder if the author was aging, and perhaps suffering from rheumatism or other ailments.

On the very next page, the handwriting changes in style. Remedies for jaundice are described, made from cucumbers, carrots and yellow doodle doo. It is impossible to say how much time may have passed between one entry and the next.

The following page begins with the words "Pour mal de Gorge" and gives a remedy for sore throat in French. The handwriting has again changed completely. From this point on, the notebook is much less orderly. Pages are skipped and entries are crossed out. The language bounces back between English and French.

Though the author changed, the purpose of the book remained the same. Most entries recorded medical recipes gathered from one doctor or another. The rest were various useful or important things.

The notebook passed from one person to another. With it, knowledge passed from one generation to the next. At the time, the rate of medical and scientific progress was slow. Cures that had roots in the alchemy of the Middle Ages would persist until new discoveries transformed our understanding of disease.

On St. Martin, passing down knowledge was mostly done orally. Wisdom and stories were preserved in memory and shared with the spoken word. Over time, the culture of St. Martin grew from this process. In this small notebook, we can see it and hold it in our hand. It has passed all the way to us.

The European cures in the notebook were abandoned long ago, but many of the plant medicine traditions passed down orally are still in use today. The sweet sage, Lippia alba, is one of dozens of plants still grown and used on St. Martin today. Illustration by Pancrace Bessa, 1827.

This rendition of the three-headed dragon of alchemy is from the 16th century text Splendor Solis by Salomon Trismosin. The three heads represent salt, sulfur and mercury. Many of the cures from this notebook were still made from the same materials, and knowledge that was hundreds of years old. Yet many people who were alive when this notebook was in use lived well into the 20th century. The changes they lived through on St. Martin must have been almost unimaginable.

The Mare Mischief

Mare Mischief took Alva on the 1st and 2nd of May, 1897

Many decades had passed for the little brown notebook before the mare Mischief arrived in its pages. The early portion of the notebook was written in the early 1800s. The sexual exploits of this horse were recorded at the end of the century.

The love life of a horse may seem out of place in a book that was mostly used to record medical remedies. On the other hand, horses were valuable, and breeding them was important. Horses transported goods and people around the island. On the plantations, they pulled cane carts or loads of other crops like tobacco and cotton.

At the Spring Plantation, the site of The Old House, records show there were 3-20 horses at any given time between the late 1700s and early 1800s. There were more horses when the plantation was profitable and fewer when it was not.

By the late 1800s, long after the peak of sugar production, the number of horses on the island may have been limited. They were valuable and surely it was expensive to import them. In the notebook, the purchase of Mischief was recorded: "Mare from Rose Duma called Mischief bought on the 5th April 1896 for 482 francs." This price would be around a couple thousand dollars in today's money.

Recording the lineage of horses may have been used to avoid interbreeding them. It could also help owners keep track of which pairs made the best offspring. This notebook doesn't record the family tree of the people writing it, but it does record the family history of the horses: "Mischief colted on the 25th April 1897 — colt called Beauty."

Mischief must have been a good horse: "mare Fanny [was] bought from Hays Viotty on the 20th March for 320 francs." Poor Fanny was only worth 2/3 the price of Mischief.

We can also see that Mischief was bred with Alva just a week after giving birth to Beauty. Mares usually go into heat about a week after giving birth. Breeding them during this "foal heat" gives the owner the chance to have a new foal each year. We don't know the rest of Mischief's story, but perhaps she still has family on St. Martin today.

Judges evaluate donkeys at what seems to be a livestock competition. For much of the 20th century, land that was no longer being farmed was used to raise livestock. These animals were used for food and transportation locally, and also exported to other islands for profit.

Father H. Smit was photographed with his carriage in front of the Roman Catholic vicarage in Philipsburg a few years before the first car arrived on St. Martin in 1914. An unnamed person holds the horse. It would be many years before cars fully replaced horses for transportation.

The Mysterious I.D. Gumbes

A handwritten index on the final page of the book gives the user a quick guide to the contents. The letter F leads to three different cures for fever and one for flux. S is for swelling, P is for pills and poultice. B is for belly ache and W for worms.

Amidst the single letters of the index is IDG for "I.D. Gumbes pills (receipt given by Dr. Allaway)." A review of page 12 reveals that these were pills "to act on the Liver." Even in this unconventional index, it would make more sense to file them under L for liver.

Who was I.D. Gumbes? This person was probably wealthy. The other people named in this notebook were mostly landowners. The people who received most European medical care at that time had money.

Like many with the name Gumbes or Gumbs, I.D. may have had a connection to Anguilla. But they surely lived on St. Martin for a while. They received a prescription from Dr. Allaway of St. Martin. The author of the notebook mentions a prescription "for my daughter Anna Gumbes." I.D. may have been her parent.

I.D. Gumbes also drew a detailed map of the Great Salt Pond and town of Philipsburg in 1847. Their name is in the bottom right corner of the map. The map is beautiful. It shows plans for a crescent-shaped dam in the pond to divert rainwater from the hills away from the salt pans. The writing on the map is clear, a mixture of pencil and ink, printing and cursive. Could it be the writing of the same person who wrote the cleanest and most careful handwriting in the little notebook?

Oddly, there doesn't seem to be any other information about I.D. Gumbes. There seems to be no record of them being born, getting married, or dying on the French side. Searchable Dutch records start later, probably after I.D. was dead. But, if their major life events happened elsewhere, records could still exist somewhere.

Though I.D. was probably wealthy and educated, we have almost no other information about this person. If we know so little about I.D., what about the poor planters and fishermen? What of the enslaved people who were the majority of St. Martiners? As more documents are digitized and shared, we will surely learn more about life on St. Martin 200 years ago. But countless stories will never be told.

A beautiful 1847 map of Philipsburg and the Great Salt Pond is the only document found so far to mention an I.D. Gumbes, aside from the notebook itself.

After the decline of the sugar industry on St. Martin, salt production was the primary industry. Numerous plans were made to boost production and efficiency at the Great Salt Pond. The map marked with I.D. Gumbes' name shows a dam (in red) that would protect the pond from rainwater. Dry season rains could ruin the year's harvest by diluting the salt pans before they could dry enough to produce salt.

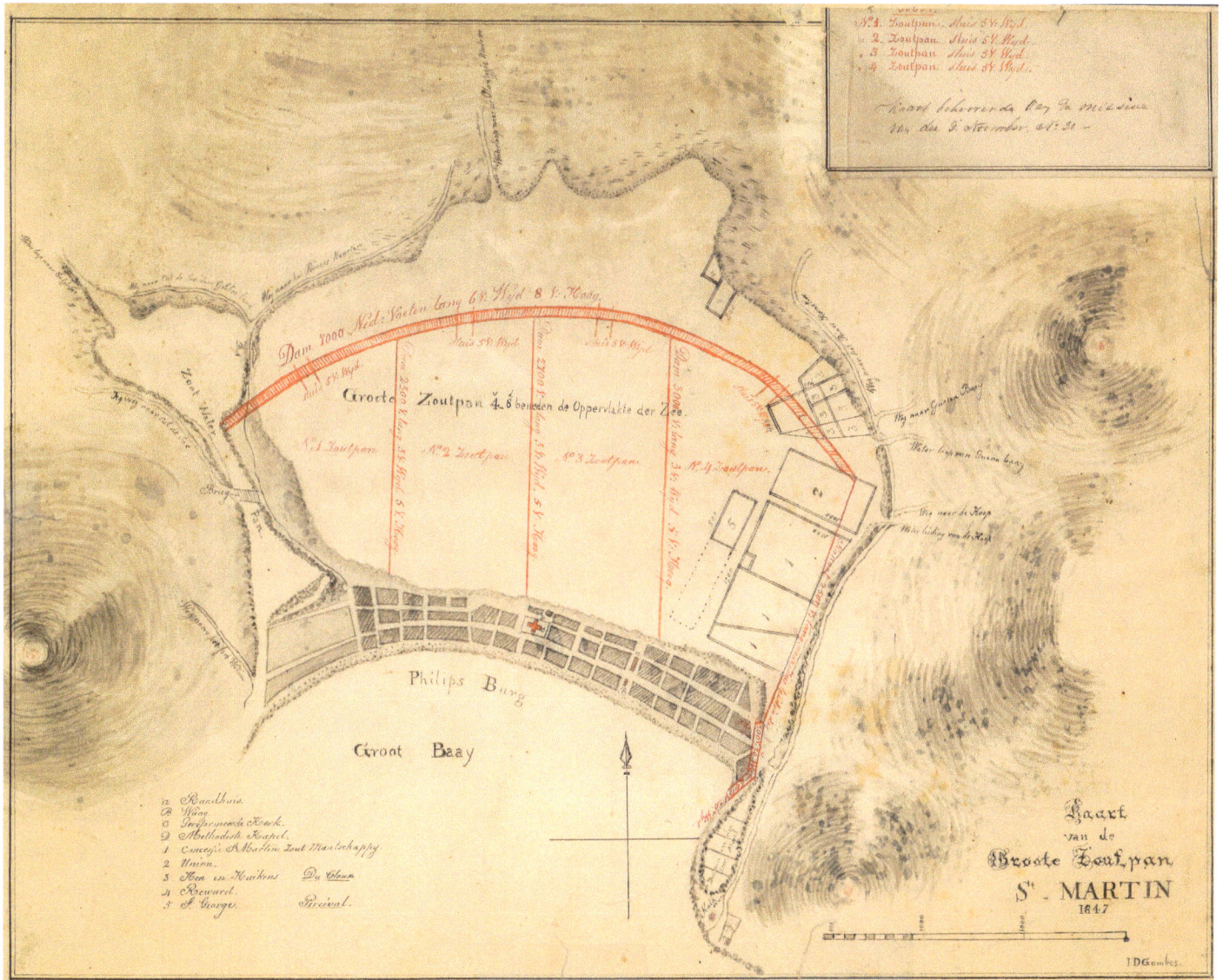

The French Years

This remarkable notebook has been protected and saved for about 200 years. Like many books of this kind, it was passed on from one person to another. Often recipe books are passed from generation to generation in the same family. Each new generation may adapt or comment on previous cures. Though this notebook had multiple authors, we don't know the relationship between them. We also don't see any comments on previous entries.

After 27 pages written in English, there is a change in handwriting. An additional 16 pages of remedies are written in a different style, primarily in French. This section begins with a remedy "Pour mal de Gorge" (for sore throat) and ends with a recipe for "Collyre" (eye drops). The eye drops seem to contain sulfur, which would burn the eyes. But they also included cocaine, so the patient wouldn't feel the burning.

The new handwriting is harder to read, and less consistent. The writing in this section may be from several people, as the ink, style and even language changes. A remedy "For putrid sore throat" appears after many pages in French and is followed by more French remedies. Pages are skipped, and in some cases remedies are included with no mention of what they are meant to treat.

The cures in this section seem to come from at least six doctors. It would be pretty surprising if there were six doctors practicing on St. Martin in the late 1800s. This was after the sugar industry had collapsed and most planters had left the island. It is possible that a number of doctors had visited the island over a period of years, and these remedies were collected that way. The changes between English and French might also reflect the language spoken by the doctor giving the cure.

One remedy for flu is attributed to a doctor "à Paris." This may mean that the the remedy came from a book by a Parisian doctor. Perhaps some of the other doctors in this section were not practicing on the island, but had published their remedies. If so, this may show a shift from learning cures directly from a doctor in the early 1800s to having access to printed materials at the end of the century.

Though more challenging to decipher, this section of the notebook surely offers more insights into life on the island and healthcare at the time. By comparing it to the earlier part of the book we may be able to learn more about how life was different between the end of the slavery era and the beginning of the Traditional Period. This tiny book, which has given us so many insights into history and culture, has more treasures to offer.

A French recipe for eye drops seems to include a sulfur compound. These eye drops would surely be painful if they didn't also include an anesthetic, cocaine.

▼ *A single page in the later section of the book contains a flu cure in French from a Parisian doctor and a remedy "For Stomach" that is written in English.*

This cure from a Dr. Shaw is written in French. The handwriting isn't easy to read, but this recipe could be be "for Victor Gumbs." If so, this may be a sign that the notebook remained in the family. Variations in how names were spelled, like Gumbes and Gumbs, were common. Victor Gumbs could easily be a descendent of Anna or I.D. Gumbes.

This book was developed as a companion to Amuseum Naturalis, St. Martin's free museum of nature, heritage and culture. The Amuseum, and this book, were created by Les Fruits de Mer.

We thank the authors of the notebook and the generations of St. Martin people who kept it safe through many gales and other unknown hardships. In particular, we thank the late Pierre Beauperthuy for his stewardship of the notebook and his dedication to St. Martin's history, heritage, culture and people.

Les Fruits de Mer is a non-profit association based in St. Martin whose core mission is to raise awareness about nature, culture, and heritage. The organization carries out this mission through a free museum, publications, films, and public events. Learn more at lesfruitsdemer.com and amuseumnaturalis.com.

AMUSEUM
NATURALIS
at The Old House

LES FRUITS DE MER